Paleolithic
diet

igloobooks

igloobooks

Published in 2015
by Igloo Books Ltd
Cottage Farm
Sywell
NN6 0BJ
www.igloobooks.com

Cover images: Thinkstock / Getty

LEO002 0415
2 4 6 8 10 9 7 5 3 1
ISBN 978-1-78440-686-8

Printed and manufactured in China

Contents

Introduction

Fed up with low energy levels, feeling sluggish and just not being as fit as you want to be? Do you want a shine to your hair and a glow to your skin? Perhaps it's time to change the way you eat – and go Paleolithic.

The Paleolithic diet takes you back to basics, eating those foods that made our forebears strong and lean. You might have heard it referred to as the caveman, hunter-gatherer, prehistoric or Stone Age diet. Whatever its name, the principle remains the same: returning to the natural goodness and nutrition that kept our ancestors in peak condition. You eat the foods that nature provides.

What is Paleolithic?

The Paleolithic diet is a balance of selected protein-rich foods (meat and fish), and vegetables and fruit. It's about enjoying fresh, healthy, toxin-free foods. It's not about calorie counting, weighing and measuring, or starving. Eating a Paleolithic diet means avoiding all dairy, processed foods and grains. On this natural diet you get your important energy-giving carbs from fruit and veg – not bread or pasta. Basically, if a food is processed, then it's not for you.

In this book, you will find all the information you need in order to get started on the Paleolithic diet. With lots of tasty recipes, lists of recommended foods, tips on eating out and your own new goals to achieve, you won't want to stop. Eating the Paleolithic way can become a long-term life choice that makes you feel good and look good. Find out how the Paleolithic approach to eating can be adapted to suit modern living. Enjoy the best of the past to make the most of the future.

All About Paleolithic

The Paleolithic diet wasn't thought of as the next wonder diet on a whim. It is based on scientific research and evidence, much of it carried out by Dr. Loren Cordain. The rationale behind the Paleolithic approach is simple: since modern man and woman are almost genetically identical to our early ancestors, why don't we return to the same principles for eating that they followed? Evidence from fossils has shown that our ancestors were lean and fit. They did not appear to suffer from many of the diseases and ailments that blight us today.

Changing foods

During the Paleolithic era, which began more than two million years ago, our hunter-gatherer ancestors ate what they could hunt and pick. About 10,000 years ago, men and women started to settle,

and began to cultivate crops and domesticate animals. Take a long jump ahead to the 18th and 19th centuries. Machinery and new agricultural products began to transform the way we produced food. Chemical fertilisers were soon used in order to grow more crops. Fast forward to today and much of what we eat is highly processed, full of preservatives and comes in a plastic wrapper or tin.

Back to the beginning

Returning to our ancestors' roots means ditching the foodstuffs that are the culprits for many of our modern health issues. Refined carbohydrates – especially sugars – and processed foods with reduced nutritional value are known to contribute to weight gain, digestive problems, mood swings and even cancer. If you want to be fit and healthy, perhaps it's time to change your diet. The Paleolithic balance of fresh fruit and vegetables with lean meat can give your body a long-term detox, and help you lose weight and look your best.

Principles and Practice

So what does a Paleolithic plate look like? The answer is simply delicious and fresh – without foods that have been processed, stripped of nutrients, or pumped full of chemicals and artificial ingredients. A typical plate will be a mixture of fresh meat and veg.

Protein will come mainly from meat, poultry, fish and eggs. Meat, oily fish, olives and seeds all supply good fats. Fruit and vegetables offer carbohydrates and a wealth of vitamins and minerals – aim for variety, so you can benefit from all their healthy nutrients.

Fish and seafood	Fruit	Nuts and seeds
Bass	Apples	Almonds
Cod	Bananas	Brazil nuts
Haddock	Berries	Cashews
Halibut	Grapes	Hazelnuts (cobnuts)
Lobster	Kiwi	Macadamia nuts
Mackerel	Mango	Pecans
Salmon	Oranges	Pine nuts
Sardines	Pineapple	Pumpkin seeds
Shrimps and prawns	Pears	Sunflower seeds
Trout	Plums	Walnuts

Veg	Meat
Artichoke	Beef
Avocado	Chicken
Aubergine (eggplant)	Duck
Broccoli	Game, such as venison
Brussels sprouts	Goat
Cabbage	Lamb
Carrots	Pork
Cauliflower	Turkey
Celery	
Courgettes (zucchini)	
Green beans (string beans)	
Radishes	
Spinach	
Sweet potatoes	
Tomatoes	

What different foods do

Here is a reminder about the function and benefits of the different food groups that feature in the Paleolithic diet.

Carbohydrate foods contain sugars and starches to provide energy in the form of glucose. In the Paleolithic diet, fruits and vegetables are your main carbohydrate sources – rather than white flour, found in bread or pasta, which has far fewer good nutrients.

Proteins are essential for the body's growth and development. They also provide energy.

Fats are an important energy source and play a key role in the body, including boosting the immune system, supporting growth and cell functions, and keeping skin and hair healthy. Fats also help your body absorb the vitamins A, D, E and K. The healthiest type are unsaturated fats from sources such as avocado, nuts and extra-virgin olive oil.

Top tips

Where possible, eat lean meat from animals fed on grass, their natural source of food. Feeding animals grain is a common practice in intensive farming and designed to bulk them up cheaply.

Fish is an excellent source of protein. Aim for three portions of oily fish a week to ensure you get plenty of healthy omega-3 fats. An alternative source are flax and hemp oils which can be consumed raw or used in cooking.

For weight loss

Fruits are a good source of vitamins and minerals. However, if you want to lose weight, avoid those containing high levels of natural sugars, especially dried fruit. Starchy veg are an excellent source of carbohydrates, but limit the amount you eat if you want to lose weight. Avoid too many nuts. Although they are protein-packed, they are calorific because they also contain high amounts of fat.

Taste

No one wants to eat tasteless food. Season dishes with garlic, onions, herbs, sea salt, ginger and pepper. A small amount of honey (high in natural sugars) is permissible, but try and go for raw local honey rather than the honey from a supermarket.

Foods to Avoid

There are some foods you need to avoid completely. Once you are eating tasty alternatives, you won't miss them.

No dairy

This includes butter, cheese, cream and milk – any by-product from a mammal.

No grains

This includes wheat (so no bread or pasta), rice, oats and other cereals.

No pulses and legumes

This includes peanuts, lentils, chickpeas, beans (kidney, mung, lima, broad and adzuki) and soya.

No refined carbs

Including: granulated sugar, high fructose corn syrup (HFCS); and grains that have been stripped of their germ and/or bran, and made 'white', in products such as white flour, white rice, white pasta and couscous.

Refined carbs

These are produced when plants that are high in carbohydrates are processed. Almost everything is taken out – including most of the fibre and nutrients – leaving just the carbohydrate (starch or sugar). The body processes this carbohydrate very quickly, causing an unhealthy, short-lived but high surge in blood glucose levels.

Eating refined, sugary foods can trigger a response in the brain associated with pleasure. That means you want to eat more of them, even though they are not benefiting your weight or health in any way. Resist temptation by having a delicious Paleolithic snack to hand.

Why?

Apart from the fact that these foods would not have been available to Paleolithic humans, there are other reasons to cut out certain foods.

Full-fat dairy foods (especially hard cheese) supply calcium but contain a lot of saturated fat, which can contribute to heart disease and stroke by increasing levels of unhealthy blood cholesterol, which then clogs and blocks arteries.

Grains contain what some call 'anti-nutrients'. These are chemicals that block the absorption of certain vitamins and minerals. Grains are lower in vitamins and minerals than meat, and they can be harder to digest.

Dr. Cordain, the first to research and create the Paleolithic diet, also suggests that pulses and legumes (peanuts, kidney beans, etc) should not be eaten because they contain high levels of anti-nutrients, which make them harder to digest.

Paleolithic Pantry

With the Paleolithic diet, you will be stocking your cupboards in a different way. You will almost certainly be cutting out certain food types that you are used to. Before you start, it's important to know that your new diet is sound and healthy, and will not deprive you of any essential nutrients.

Key calcium

One of the main food groups you will lose is dairy. You may be concerned that if you are not eating dairy products you will not get enough calcium, which is crucial for healthy strong bones. Well, worry no longer. Prehistoric humans did not drink cow's milk. The gene which helps us digest it developed only with the advent of farming. In many parts of the world today, only infants drink milk, and a significant proportion of adults cannot digest its key enzyme: lactose.

Alternative sources of calcium include salmon and sardines, both of which are also rich in vitamin D, which helps the body use calcium effectively. Other calcium sources include broccoli and kale, although the calcium from vegetables is less easily absorbed. Eating nuts and seeds will boost your calcium intake, too.

Make sure you spend time outdoors and get plenty of sunlight, just as our prehistoric ancestors did. Sunlight helps calcium absorption because its UVB rays prompt the body to produce its own vitamin D.

Calcium-rich Paleolithic foods

- almonds

- bones (use to make stock)

- broccoli

- cress

- eggs

- green beans (string beans)

- sardines (with bones)

- shrimp

Drinks

While you are eating nature's best, drink it too! Water is crucial for health so make sure you drink plenty. Avoid sweet fizzy drinks as they supply calories from sugar but little else.

A word on supplements

If you have a balanced diet, you shouldn't need to take supplements. However, this is a personal choice, depending on your individual needs and circumstances.

Clearing out

Now it's time to clear out your cupboards and put away the foods you know you are not going to eat (flour, sugar, pasta etc.) into one corner, hidden from sight. Much as you may have liked them, remember that these are the highly processed products that run counter to all the main principles of eating the Paleolithic way.

During processing, many foods are stripped of fibre and important nutrients, such as vitamins and minerals. Chemical additives and preservatives are often introduced and do very little for your nutritional health.

As a reminder, stick a list of the foods you can eat on your fridge – there are plenty of them!

Stocking up

When you first start on the Paleolithic diet, you may be more conscious of the foods you can't eat than the ones you can. Plan ahead so that the urge for a bagel or wrap doesn't take you by surprise. Look at the Eating Out tips on page 24 and the ideas on pages 124–127. Use up leftovers to best effect. For instance, if you cook a chicken, make stock from the carcass. You can freeze it and use it in another dish or as the basis of a tasty soup.

Go shopping with a list and a plan of your weekly meals. If possible, encourage others in your household to join you in this diet. If you do most of the cooking, introduce some Paleolithic meals. Amid so many delicious, fresh tastes, other family members may not even notice missing ingredients, such as bread.

Take a look at the recipes in this book – they will supply all the meals you require from breakfast through to supper, including snacks.

Questions of cost

Some people say that this is an expensive diet because all the ingredients are fresh. But if you plan ahead, it need not be a costly way of eating – and the nutritional benefit you get from fresh ingredients will far outweigh any added expense. When it comes to good food, fresh beats processed every time.

Blueberries

Chicken breast

Broccoli

Carrots

Brazil nuts

Get Healthy

You are what you eat – and your appearance reflects that. Skin and hair will glow and shine with the Paleolithic diet, rich in fresh fruit and veg, lots of natural proteins, natural oils and natural sugars.

Protein push

Protein makes up about 20 per cent of your body weight. It's what keeps your muscles in peak order, your nails strong, your hair thick and shiny, your skin glowing and your eyes sparkly. Proteins are a key part of the cells in your internal organs, including your heart muscle and brain.

Common questions

I'm a vegetarian. Can I follow this diet?

It's very hard to follow the Paleolithic diet if you are vegetarian or vegan as you need to eat lots of meat and fish for protein. Remember you don't eat any dairy foods, beans and pulses, or processed proteins such as soya, all of which are often staples of a vegetarian diet.

I'm in training. Will I get enough energy from Paleolithic foods?

Yes, replace those stodgy energy-giving pasta meals with vegetables such as sweet potatoes and yams, and fruits such as bananas.

Proteins are made up of 22 amino acids. The body needs these but cannot make all of them. The ones that the body does not make are found in Paleolithic foods such as meat, poultry, fish and eggs.

Feeling good

The aim of this diet is to help you look good and feel good. Follow its basic principles but don't worry about sticking to the rules 100 per cent of the time. Most people cannot buy only grass-fed organic beef due to budget and lack of availability in the supermarkets. If you can't get fully organic food or grass-fed meat, choose the closest alternative. Be realistic so that the diet is manageable.

Mind Over Matter

Let's be realistic. Any diet that is going to last more than a week and has long-term benefits needs to work for today's busy people. With the Paleolithic diet, you should aim to eat according to Paleolithic principles about 80 per cent of the time, and, for convenience, allow yourself to eat more freely for the other 20 per cent.

It's best to get started on a strict routine so that you reap the maximum rewards in the first few weeks. You can then become a bit more flexible.

Make it work

Use the Paleolithic principles so that they work for you. If your goal is weight loss, stick to the diet rigidly until you are near to your ideal weight, and avoid too many starchy vegetables, such as sweet potatoes, or high-sugar fruits.

When you have achieved your desired weight, you will probably want to continue with the diet, but then you can add starchier vegetables and nuts.

Adapt your approach to Paleolithic eating according to your needs. For instance, if you plan to undertake a triathlon and want more energy, make sure you bulk up on starchy vegetables before an event. Once you have started to eat Paleolithic, and have seen and felt the results, you won't want to stop.

Goals

Think about what you want to achieve from this diet. It may be weight loss or it may be to rediscover the energy that has been sapped by too much junk food. Perhaps you just want to feel more connected to the food you eat. Whatever your motivation, set yourself some goals. Then you can measure your progress.

Eating Out

Everyone likes to socialise and chat with a friend over a coffee, or have people round for dinner. It's easier to manage the Paleolithic diet if you are cooking – and it's a great way to encourage others to join the growing Paleolithic community! It's trickier to manage if someone else is entertaining you in their home. No one wants to reject the host's food simply because the fish is swimming in a sea of butter.

Top tips

If possible, mention to a host beforehand that you prefer not to eat dairy or grains. That way, he or she can provide a meal – or options – that avoid both.

In a restaurant, choose simply cooked food, without sauces. Obviously, going to an outlet that only sells pies or pizza is not going to work for you (unless that is your 20 per cent).

- Eat before you go out, so you are not overly hungry and then you won't be tempted to tuck into bread and butter on the table.

- Choose restaurants carefully. Fast-food outlets are unlikely to use olive oil, but other restaurants are.

- Call the restaurant in advance to ask if it is possible to order off the menu.

- Choose a gluten-free option so you know you won't be getting grains.

- Order a selection of vegetables as a main course.

What to drink?

As you know, water is best, but even sparkling water has its limitations for a special occasion! A glass of red or white wine will do no harm. Avoid grain-based drinks such as beer and also spirits, such as whisky, that are made from grains. Don't add sugary mixers. Avoid caffeinated drinks such as coffee and tea – choose herbal teas instead.

Get Fit

The beauty of eating the Paleolithic way is that you don't have to count calories or weigh foods to exact measurements – but you will lose weight. As you cut out fatty meats, dairy foods, sugar and all the empty calories in processed foods, you are already on the road to fitness. You can eat a sensible amount so you don't feel hungry, which means you are more likely to stick with eating Paleolithic than other diets. It becomes a lifestyle.

All-round fitness

Fitness isn't just about weight. It's about a toned body and sharp mind. Without all the sugar and chemical toxins from processed foods conspiring to keep your blood glucose yo-yoing from high to low, you will feel more balanced and alert.

Every diet is more effective when matched with a sensible exercise routine. After starting on the Paleolithic diet, you will want to take the stairs instead of the escalator, walk instead of drive, and get into sporting action.

Get started

Take some time to think about how you are going to get started on this new approach to food and fitness. Choose an achievable exercise programme and timetable to make sure it works for you. Soon, the combination of Paleolithic eating plus exercise will give you more energy and improve your fitness. Try not to be driven by weighing scales – the way you look and feel is a better gauge.

Active and Fit

You will not reap the greatest rewards from a healthy Paleolithic diet if you never exercise. To boost your fitness and health, every diet needs to be accompanied by a sensible activity plan.

Fresh food, fresh air

- Buddy up with a friend and nip out to the park for a 20-minute jog. Or take up a team sport. Netball, football, or badminton all provide a great workout and plenty of fun, too. Don't be put off by not knowing the rules or thinking you won't be any good – everyone is a beginner at some point.

- A brisk daily walk will get your pulse going, and give your legs and bum a good workout.

- Swimming is an excellent all-round exercise. If it's summer and you don't like chlorinated indoor pools, consider joining a 'wild' swimming group to swim in lakes and rivers.

- Join a dance class. Don't worry about your sense of rhythm or remembering steps – what's important is enjoyment.

- Try a yoga class – yoga stretches the muscles that few other exercises reach.

- Dust down your old bike, fix the brakes and ride. Cycle to work, to see friends or just for the sheer pleasure. You can pick up second-hand bikes easily and cheaply.

- Join a gym and work out.

Exercise benefits

Exercise helps you lose weight, and tones and trims your body. It also makes you feel good as it triggers the release of hormones called endorphins that give you a natural high.

Aim to exercise for at least 40 minutes – three times a week – add it into your weekly plan.

Keeping Motivated

To help you stick to your diet, think about the goals you set yourself (see pages 22–23). Then use the charts on pages 114–121 to record how you're doing.

Before you start, check your weight, and note your energy and mood levels, giving them a score from 0–10. Use the charts to plan your meals for four weeks, and to record your weight, your exercise activities and how you feel – again rating your energy and mood on the 0–10 scale. By comparing your readings, you will be able to measure the Paleolithic effect.

If, after four weeks, you want to continue monitoring your progress, note your weight, energy and mood levels in a diary to assess the longer-term effect.

Need a boost?

Had a bad day at work? Fed up with juggling several balls to meet impossible demands? That's the time you would probably have turned to a chocolate bar or headed off to the nearest fast food outlet for a burger, bun and sweet fizzy drink.

Don't! If you are going to eat non-Paleolithic, make sure it's a food that still provides nourishment and satisfies. Or choose a Paleolithic sweet snack (see page 94) that will lift your mood but not leave you in the doldrums minutes later.

Dealing with cravings

Any new diet is challenging as your body adjusts to different foods. Try to manage your cravings and stay Paleolithic. If you long for particular foods, work out what your body is missing and replace it with some extra amounts from your Paleolithic menu. Perhaps you are not eating enough starchy vegetables and fruit to satisfy the need for carbohydrates. If you crave sugar, add in a honey-laced snack (remembering to use local raw honey if possible). You can follow a rigid Paleolithic diet or you can follow the principles but be practical and occasionally use small amounts of other ingredients. In this book we have included nut flours and a few other non-Paleolithic ingredients. Choose what works for you.

Health Aware

It's always a good idea to check with your doctor before starting a new eating regimen. This is essential if you have any medical issues, have ever had an eating disorder, or are pregnant or breastfeeding.

This plan is ideal if you follow a gluten-free diet because you cannot tolerate gluten. Gluten is the name given to the proteins in wheat. It acts like glue in baked goods, enabling ingredients to bind together. For those with coeliac disease, eating gluten produces an immune reaction, leading to inflammation in the small intestine.

Other people have a gluten sensitivity and find that eating gluten gives them digestive problems and makes them feel sluggish. If you think you may have either condition, see your doctor before starting this diet. It is important not to eliminate wheat until your doctor has established the exact cause of the problem.

If you are – or suspect you may be – lactose intolerant, the Paleolithic diet is also ideal for you, because it contains no dairy foods.

Listen to your body

Keep a careful note of your mood and energy levels (see pages 30–31). Once you have started this diet, you are likely to feel both fitter and more alert. If you also cut out caffeine, you may experience some headaches initially for a few days – instant evidence of the addictive effect of caffeine – but these should quickly subside. When you exercise, remember to warm up and cool down. Take time to listen to your body. If something doesn't feel right, stop and get it checked.

Breakfasts and Brunches

Breakfast is the easiest meal to skip but the most important. It sets you up for the day. A Paleolithic breakfast supplies slow-release energy that lasts until lunchtime, and stops you reaching for an unhealthy snack.

As sugary cereals, porridge or toast are out, it's time to get creative. Choose Paleolithic nut breads or brioche, and make your own granola with seeds, nuts and dried fruit.

A cup of hot water with a slice of lime or lemon is a perfect refreshing and detoxifying drink for the start of the day. Or make fresh herb tea with mint leaves infused in hot water.

When you don't have to rush, treat yourself to a leisurely brunch. Invite friends round to share a morning feast, such as pancakes or a soufflé with delicious fruit smoothies.

Read on and enjoy breakfast as never before.

Almond Flour Pancakes

Serves: 4
Preparation time: 10 minutes
Cooking time: 25–30 minutes

Ingredients

300 g / 10 ½ oz / 2 cups strawberries, hulled
  and chopped

150 g / 5 oz / 1 cup almond flour, sifted

a pinch of salt

2 large eggs, beaten

250 ml / 9 fl. oz / 1 cup almond milk

55 g / 2 oz / ¼ cup grass-fed butter, melted

Method

1. Place the strawberries in a saucepan with
   1 tbsp of water. Cook over a medium heat,
   stirring occasionally, until softened
   and juicy.

2. Combine the flour and salt in a bowl.
   Whisk in the eggs, then add the milk
   gradually until smooth.

3. Add 1 tbsp of melted butter; whisk and
   leave for 15 minutes.

4. Heat a pan over a medium heat and grease
   with melted butter. Add a small ladle of
   batter to the centre of the pan.

5. Cook for 1 minute, until set, then flip and
   cook for a further 30 seconds. Slide onto
   a plate and cook the remaining pancakes
   following the same method.

6. Serve with stewed strawberries.

Asparagus Smoothies

Serves: 4
Preparation time: 10–15 minutes

Ingredients

8 large white asparagus spears, trimmed and chopped

150 ml / 5 fl. oz / ⅔ cup almond milk

250 g / 9 oz / 1 cup crushed ice

12 large green asparagus spears, trimmed and chopped

2 Granny Smith apples, peeled, cored and chopped

55 g / 2 oz / 1 cup baby spinach, washed

Method

1. Place the white asparagus, almond milk and half of the ice in a blender; blitz until smooth and then pour into a jug.

2. Combine the remaining ice with the green asparagus, apple and spinach in the blender; blitz until smooth.

3. Pour the green asparagus smoothie into glasses before slowly pouring the white asparagus smoothie on top.

Steamed Beef Meatballs

Serves: 4
Preparation time:
10 minutes plus chilling
Cooking time: 35–45 minutes

Ingredients

600 g / 1 lb 5 oz / 4 cups lean steak mince
a small bunch of coriander (cilantro), chopped
1 large egg
55 g / 2 oz / ½ cup ground almonds
salt and freshly ground black pepper
100 g / 3 ½ oz / ½ cup ready-made
   Paleolithic chilli (chili) sauce

Method

1. Combine the steak mince, most of the coriander, egg, ground almonds and seasoning in a large mixing bowl.

2. Mix together with your hands until thoroughly combined; cover and chill for 15 minutes.

3. Bring a half-filled saucepan of water to a simmer.

4. Shape the mixture into meatballs between the palms of your hands, then arrange the meatballs, spaced apart, in a large steaming basket.

5. Cover and steam for 30–40 minutes until firm and cooked through. Serve with the remaining coriander and some chilli sauce on the side.

Orange Walnut Bread

Serves: 8
Preparation time: 10 minutes
Cooking time: 25–35 minutes

Ingredients

1 large courgette (zucchini), grated

5 large eggs, separated

150 g / 5 oz / 1 cup walnut flour

¼ tsp cream of tartar

½ tsp salt

1 large orange, thinly sliced

Method

1. Preheat the oven to 180°C (160°C fan) / 350F / gas 4, then grease and line a 900 g (2 lb) loaf tin with greaseproof paper.

2. Mix together the courgette and egg yolks in a large bowl; beat well until combined.

3. Fold the flour and cream of tartar into the mixture until combined.

4. Beat the egg whites with the salt in a separate mixing bowl until stiffly peaked, then fold into the egg yolk and courgette mixture. Spoon into the loaf tin.

5. Top with the slices of orange and bake for 25–35 minutes until golden and risen. Remove to a wire rack to cool before turning out and serving.

Prune Bread Fingers

Serves: 8
Preparation time: 10–15 minutes
Cooking time: 25–30 minutes

Ingredients

175 g / 6 oz / ¾ cup almond butter

6 medium eggs

1 tbsp raw honey

55 ml / 2 fl. oz / ¼ cup coconut oil, melted

½ tbsp white wine vinegar

55 g / 2 oz / ⅓ cup walnut flour

1 tsp baking powder

½ tsp salt

400 g / 14 oz / 2 cups canned prunes, drained

55 g / 2 oz / ½ cup golden flax or linseeds

Method

1. Preheat the oven to 180°C (160°C fan) / 350F / gas 4. Line a large baking tray with greaseproof paper.

2. Beat together the almond butter, eggs, honey, coconut oil and vinegar until smooth.

3. Add the walnut flour, baking powder and salt, mixing well.

4. Spoon the mixture into finger shapes on the baking tray, then stud with prunes and the seeds.

5. Bake for 25–30 minutes until golden and slightly risen. Remove to a wire rack to cool before serving.

Almond Brioche

Serves: 8
Preparation time:
  25 minutes plus proving
Cooking time: 35–45 minutes

Ingredients

150 g / 5 oz / 1 cup almond flour

150 g / 5 oz / 1 cup coconut flour

1 ½ tsp dried active yeast

½ tsp salt

150 ml / 5 fl. oz / ⅔ cup almond milk

110 ml / 4 fl. oz / 1 cup sparkling water

2 small eggs

75 g / 3 oz / ⅓ cup raw honey

100 g / 3 ½ oz / ½ cup almond butter

1 tbsp whole almonds

Method

1. Combine the flours, yeast and salt in a bowl, then whisk together the almond milk, water, eggs, honey and almond butter in a jug.

2. Add the wet ingredients to the dry and mix well until a dough forms.

3. Transfer to a clean bowl; cover with a damp towel and leave to rise in a warm place for 2 hours.

4. Preheat the oven to 180°C (160°C fan) / 350F / gas 4 and then line a 900 g (2 lb) pudding dish with greaseproof paper.

5. Shape the dough into the dish and top with almonds; prove for a further 30 minutes in a warm place.

6. Bake for 35–45 minutes until golden. Allow to cool before serving.

Melon Smoothie

Serves: 4
Preparation time: 5 minutes

Ingredients

1 medium Cantaloupe melon, diced
1 lime, juiced
a pinch of salt
250 g / 9 oz / 1 cup crushed ice

Method

1. Combine the melon flesh, lime juice, salt and ice in a food processor or blender.

2. Blend until smooth.

3. Pour into glasses and serve immediately.

Chestnut Flour Pancakes

Serves: 4
Preparation time:
10 minutes plus resting
Cooking time: 20–25 minutes

Ingredients

600 g / 1 lb 5 oz / 4 cups Bramley apples,
 peeled, cored and finely diced

2 tbsp water

150 g / 5 oz / 1 cup chestnut flour

a pinch of salt

2 large eggs, beaten

250 ml / 9 fl. oz / 1 cup coconut milk

55 g / 2 oz / ¼ cup grass-fed butter, melted

Method

1. Cook the apple with the water in a saucepan set over a medium heat; once soft, set to one side.

2. Combine the flour and salt in a large mixing bowl. Whisk in the eggs and then gradually whisk in the coconut milk.

3. Whisk in 1 tbsp of melted butter; leave to rest for 10 minutes.

4. Heat a pan over a medium heat and grease with melted butter. Add a small ladle of batter to the centre of the pan.

5. Cook for 1 minute, until set, then flip and cook for a further 30 seconds and then slide onto a plate. Repeat this method for the remaining pancakes.

6. Serve the pancakes with stewed apple.

Coriander Meatballs

Serves: 4
Preparation time:
  10–15 minutes plus chilling
Cooking time: 20–25 minutes

Ingredients

1 large red onion
600 g / 1 lb 5 oz / 4 cups pork mince
a large bunch of coriander (cilantro), chopped
2 cloves of garlic, minced
2 tbsp almonds, chopped
salt and freshly ground black pepper
110 g / 4 oz / ½ cup dairy-free
  coconut milk yoghurt
½ tsp Madras curry powder
a pinch of cumin seeds
1 gem lettuce, leaves separated
1 large tomato, chopped

Method

1. Finely chop most of the onion and place in a bowl; slice the remainder and reserve.

2. Add the pork mince, most of the coriander, garlic, almonds and seasoning to the chopped red onion. Mix together until thoroughly combined. Cover and chill for 15 minutes.

3. Preheat the oven to 190°C (170°C fan) / 375F / gas 5 and line a large baking tray with greaseproof paper.

4. Shape the mixture into meatballs between your palms. Arrange on the tray, spaced apart, and bake for 20–25 minutes until firm and starting to brown.

5. Spoon the yoghurt into pots and top with curry powder, cumin seeds and the remaining coriander. Serve alongside the meatballs, lettuce, tomato and sliced onion.

Chestnut Spread

Serves: 4
Preparation time: 15 minutes
Cooking time: 25 minutes

Ingredients

400 g / 14 oz / 2 cups chestnuts

2 tbsp water

1 tbsp raw honey

½ tsp vanilla extract

Method

1. Score the undersides of the chestnuts with a small paring knife. Place in a saucepan and cover with water.

2. Bring to boiling point and cook for 18–20 minutes until soft; drain and leave to cool.

3. Once cool enough to handle, peel and combine with the water, honey and vanilla extract in a food processor.

4. Blend until smooth. Scrape into a container, cover, and chill until ready to serve.

Omelette Soufflé

Serves: 4
Preparation time: 5–10 minutes
Cooking time: 15 minutes

Ingredients

8 large eggs, separated
150 ml / 5 fl. oz / ⅔ cup almond milk
salt and freshly ground pepper
2 tbsp grass-fed butter, melted
a few sprigs of thyme, to garnish
1 lemon, cut into wedges

Method

1. Preheat the grill to a moderate heat. Beat the egg yolks with the almond milk and plenty of salt and pepper in a mixing bowl.

2. Beat the egg whites in a separate bowl with a pinch of salt until stiffly peaked. Add a quarter to the egg yolk mixture and whisk well before gently folding in the remainder.

3. Heat a little melted butter in an omelette pan set over a moderate heat until hot. Add a quarter of the egg mixture and cook for 1 minute until set before transferring to the grill.

4. Finish cooking for 2 minutes until puffed and brown; repeat for the remaining omelettes.

5. Serve with sprigs of thyme and lemon wedges.

Chicken-stuffed Tomatoes

Serves: 4
Preparation time: 15 minutes
Cooking time: 35–40 minutes

Ingredients

600 g / 1 lb 5 oz / 4 cups skinless, boneless
   chicken thighs

2 large onions, chopped

2 cloves of garlic, chopped

4 beef tomatoes

75 g / 3 oz / ¾ cup pine nuts

3 tbsp olive oil

salt and freshly ground black pepper

Method

1. Preheat the oven to 190°C (170°C fan) /
   375F / gas 5.

2. Pulse together the chicken meat, onion,
   and garlic with plenty of seasoning until
   finely chopped.

3. Remove the tops of the tomatoes and
   reserve, then scoop out most of the flesh
   and seeds.

4. Fill the cavities with the chicken stuffing.
   Top with pine nuts and replace the tops of
   the tomatoes over the filling.

5. Arrange in a baking or roasting dish and
   drizzle with olive oil. Bake for 35–40
   minutes until soft and the skins are
   wrinkled.

Watermelon Mint Smoothie

Serves: 4
Preparation time: 10 minutes

Ingredients

½ small watermelon, diced
½ lemon, juiced
a small bunch of mint, picked
250 g / 9 oz / 1 cup crushed ice

Method

1. Combine the watermelon flesh, lemon juice, a small handful of mint leaves and ice in a food processor or blender.
2. Blend until smooth, then pour into glasses and serve with more mint to garnish.

Artichoke Omelette

Serves: 4
Preparation time: 10–15 minutes
Cooking time: 25–30 minutes

Ingredients

12 small eggs

150 ml / 5 fl. oz / ⅔ cup almond milk

flaked sea salt and freshly ground black pepper

2 tbsp olive oil

2 globe artichokes, peeled with stems intact

1 tsp dried basil

1 tsp dried oregano

a small bunch of basil, leaves picked

Method

1. Preheat the oven to 180°C (160°C fan) / 350F / gas 4.

2. Beat together the eggs with the milk and plenty of salt and freshly ground black pepper.

3. Grease a rectangular baking dish with the olive oil, then pour in the egg mixture.

4. Split the artichokes in half and arrange, 'top and tailed,' in the dish.

5. Sprinkle over the dried herbs. Bake for 20–25 minutes until the artichokes are tender to the point of a knife.

6. Remove from the oven and leave to cool briefly before garnishing with basil leaves and serving. Season with sea salt and pepper.

Apple Hazelnut Compote

Serves: 4
Preparation time: 15 minutes
Cooking time: 20–25 minutes

Ingredients

1 kg / 2 lb 4 oz / 6 ⅔ cups Bramley apples, peeled, cored and diced

2 tbsp water

½ lemon, juiced

2 tbsp raw honey

55 g / 2 oz / ½ cup hazelnuts (cobnuts), crushed

Method

1. Combine the apple, water, lemon juice and honey in a large saucepan.

2. Bring to a simmer over a moderate heat, then cover and cook over a reduced heat for 12–15 minutes until very soft.

3. Scrape into a food processor and blend until smooth. Leave to cool, then spoon into serving glasses.

4. Top with crushed hazelnuts before serving.

Stewed Pears

Serves: 4
Preparation time: 5 minutes
Cooking time: 20–25 minutes

Ingredients

900 g / 2 lb / 6 cups ripe pears, peeled, cored and diced

2 tbsp water

2 tbsp raw honey

½ tsp vanilla extract

a small handful of mint leaves, chopped

Method

1. Combine the pear, water, honey and vanilla extract in a large saucepan.

2. Bring to a simmer over a medium heat, then cover and cook over a reduced heat for 15–20 minutes until the pear is very soft.

3. Leave to cool before spooning into bowls and serving with a garnish of mint.

Light Bites and Lunches

Too often, lunch is a quick sandwich grabbed on the run. With a little planning and preparation, you can make it a nutritious and easy part of the Paleolithic programme.

Blitz vegetables and herbs to make a soup. Invest in a thermos flask to keep it hot for chilly winter days, or ice cold and fresh for blazing summer days. Experiment too, with this fresh range of Paleolithic salads – all of them are packed wit h wholesome ingredients providing optimal nutrition.

Accompany with water – sparkling or still – or a smoothie from your breakfast range. A slice of breakfast nut bread will also make a lighter salad a little more substantial.

Mix and match the lunch and light bite ideas in this section, for a varied and substantial meal. Enjoy!

Cold Beef Salad

Serves: 4
Preparation time: 10 minutes

Ingredients

55 g / 2 oz / ¼ cup grass-fed butter, softened

1 tbsp golden linseeds

½ shallot, finely chopped

salt and freshly ground black pepper

4 large spring onions (scallions), sliced

6 large cooked beetroot in vinegar, drained and diced

2 tbsp olive oil

1 tbsp sesame seeds

600 g / 1 lb 5 oz / 4 cups roast beef, cold

75 g / 3 oz / 1 ½ cups watercress, roughly chopped

Method

1. Mash together the softened butter with the linseeds, shallot, salt and pepper. Chill until needed.

2. Toss the spring onion and beetroot with the olive oil, sesame seeds and seasoning.

3. Spoon onto plates. Slice the beef and lay it on top, then garnish with watercress.

4. Serve with the butter on top.

Chicken Yakitori Salad

Serves: 4
Preparation time:
  20 minutes plus marinating
Cooking time: 10 minutes

Ingredients

55 ml / 2 fl. oz / ¼ cup fish sauce

2 tbsp wheat-free tamari sauce

4 skinless chicken breasts, diced

½ Galia melon

1 red pepper, deseeded and finely diced

2 kiwi fruit, peeled and diced

150 g / 5 oz / 3 cups mixed leaf salad

a small bunch of mint leaves, picked

8 wooden skewers, soaked in cold water for
  15 minutes beforehand

freshly ground mixed peppercorns

Method

1. Whisk together the fish sauce and tamari sauce in a bowl. Add half to the diced chicken in a separate bowl and stir well to coat.

2. Leave to marinate for 15 minutes. Meanwhile, preheat the grill to hot.

3. Thread the marinated chicken onto the skewers and arrange on a grilling tray; season with freshly ground pepper.

4. Grill for 7–8 minutes, turning occasionally, until golden and firm to the touch.

5. Use a melon baller to scoop out balls of melon; toss with the pepper, kiwi fruit, mixed leaf salad and mint leaves.

6. Serve the yakitori chicken skewers with the salad on the side and the remaining marinade for dipping.

Marinated Salmon Salad

Serves: 4
Preparation time:
   15 minutes plus chilling
Calories/serving: 173

Ingredients

450 g / 1 lb / 3 cups skinless salmon fillet

2 lemons, juiced

a small bunch of dill, chopped

150 g / 5 oz / 3 cups rocket (arugula), washed

100 g / 3 ½ oz / ½ cup dairy-free
   coconut milk yoghurt

1 tsp red peppercorns, lightly crushed

salt and freshly ground black pepper

Method

1. Finely slice the salmon into strips; toss with the lemon juice and seasoning in a bowl.

2. Cover and chill for 15 minutes before stirring through most of the chopped dill.

3. Arrange the rocket on plates and top with the marinated salmon.

4. Whisk together the coconut yoghurt with the remaining dill and some seasoning.

5. Spoon over the salmon before garnishing with the peppercorns and serving.

Chicken Salad

Serves: 4
Preparation time: 10–15 minutes
Cooking time: 10 minutes

Ingredients

4 skinless chicken breasts, cut into strips
55 ml / 2 fl. oz / ¼ cup coconut oil, melted
1 red cabbage, shredded
75 g / 3 oz / 1 cup radishes, sliced
2 small Gala apples, cored and thinly sliced
75 g / 3 oz / 1 ½ cups lamb's lettuce
a small bunch of chives, finely chopped
salt and freshly ground black pepper

Method

1. Preheat the grill to hot. Brush the chicken strips with coconut oil and season with salt and pepper.

2. Arrange on a tray and grill for 8–10 minutes, turning once halfway through, until golden and cooked through.

3. Meanwhile, toss together the cabbage, radish, apple, lamb's lettuce and chives in a large mixing bowl; season with salt and pepper.

4. Divide the salad between plates and top with the grilled chicken, then serve.

Grilled Squid Salad

Serves: 4
Preparation time: 10–15 minutes
Cooking time: 10 minutes

Ingredients

1 squid, washed and dried

2 tbsp coconut oil, melted

2 tsp smoked paprika

a pinch of Cayenne pepper

4 salad tomatoes, chopped

300 g / 10 ½ oz / 2 cups preserved red peppers in oil, drained and chopped

110 g / 4 oz / ⅔ cup black olives

100 g / 3 ½ oz / 2 cups frisée lettuce

salt and freshly ground black pepper

Method

1. Preheat the grill to a moderately hot temperature. Prepare the squid into bite-sized pieces with a sharp knife.

2. Pat dry then drizzle with oil and seasoning with paprika, Cayenne, salt and pepper.

3. Arrange on a tray and grill for 6–7 minutes, turning occasionally, until golden and cooked through.

4. Toss together the tomatoes, peppers, olives and frisée. Arrange in bowls and top with the grilled squid before serving.

Asparagus Pork Salad

Serves: 4
Preparation time: 10 minutes
Cooking time: 5 minutes

Ingredients

100 g / 3 ½ oz / ½ cup dairy-free
coconut milk yoghurt

1 tsp Dijon mustard

1 tbsp hot water

½ tsp paprika

450 g / 1 lb / 4 cups asparagus spears,
woody ends removed

150 g / 5 oz / 1 cup roast pork slices

2 tbsp baby capers in brine, drained

a large handful of rocket (arugula)

salt and freshly ground black pepper

Method

1. Whisk together the yoghurt, mustard, hot
   water and paprika in a small bowl; season
   and set to one side.

2. Cook the asparagus in a large saucepan of
   salted, boiling water for 3–4 minutes until
   tender; refresh immediately in iced water.

3. Once cool, drain, pat dry and arrange
   on plates.

4. Top with folded slices of pork, baby capers
   and rocket leaves; dress with the yoghurt
   sauce and a little more seasoning
   before serving.

Apple Herring Salad

Serves: 4
Preparation time: 15 minutes

Ingredients

a small bunch of chives

75 g / 3 oz / ⅓ cup dairy-free
  coconut milk yoghurt

400 g / 14 oz / 2 ⅔ cups pickled herring fillet,
  diced

4 Granny Smith apples, peeled,
  cored and diced

75 g / 3 oz / ⅓ cup pickled ginger root,
  shaved

2 tsp red peppercorns, lightly crushed

salt and freshly ground black pepper

Method

1. Finely chop a few chive stalks. Whisk with
   the coconut yoghurt and seasoning until
   smooth before setting to one side.

2. Toss the herring fillet with the apple,
   shaved ginger and seasoning.

3. Spoon onto plates and drizzle with a little
   of the coconut yoghurt dressing. Garnish
   with peppercorns and the remaining
   chives before serving.

Grilled Chicken Salad

Serves: 4
Preparation time: 10 minutes
Cooking time: 20 minutes

Ingredients

4 skinless chicken breasts, trimmed

75 ml / 3 fl. oz / ⅓ cup olive oil

100 g / 3 ½ oz / 2 cups lamb's lettuce, torn

55 g / 2 oz / 1 cup baby spinach

½ Cantaloupe melon, prepared into balls

1 tbsp balsamic vinegar

salt and freshly ground black pepper

Method

1. Preheat the grill to a moderately hot temperature. Drizzle the chicken breasts with a little olive oil, then season generously.

2. Arrange on a tray and grill for 16–18 minutes until golden and firm to the touch, turning occasionally. They should register at least 71°C / 160F on a meat thermometer.

3. Remove the chicken from the grill and leave to rest briefly. Serve with the lamb's lettuce, spinach and melon balls.

4. Mix the remaining olive oil with the balsamic vinegar and drizzle a little over the salad, serving the remainder on the side.

Crab Salad Appetisers

Serves: 4
Preparation time: 10 minutes

Ingredients

350 g / 12 oz / 2 ⅓ cups canned white
    crabmeat

1 red chilli (chili), finely sliced

4 spring onions (scallions), finely sliced

55 g / 2 oz / ½ cup almonds, chopped

a large bunch of flat-leaf parsley, chopped

2 tbsp olive oil

1 lemon, juiced

2 gem lettuce, large leaves separated

salt and freshly ground black pepper

Method

1. Combine the crabmeat, chilli, spring onion,
   almonds and chopped parsley with the
   olive oil, lemon juice and seasoning.

2. Stir well to bind before spooning into the
   larger lettuce leaves.

3. Serve chilled.

Chicken Liver Salad

Serves: 4
Preparation time: 10–15 minutes
Cooking time: 20 minutes

Ingredients

450 g / 1 lb / 3 cups chicken livers, washed

250 ml / 9 fl. oz / 1 cup light coconut milk

300 g / 10 ½ oz / 2 cups baby potatoes, halved

2 tbsp coconut oil, melted

2 cloves of garlic, sliced

200 g / 7 oz / 1 ⅓ cups cherry tomatoes, halved

100 g / 3 ½ oz / 2 cups mixed leaf salad

a small handful of tarragon leaves, chopped

150 g / 5 oz / ⅔ cup dairy-free coconut milk yoghurt

1 tsp wholegrain mustard

salt and freshly ground black pepper

Method

1. Soak the chicken livers in the milk for 15 minutes; cover and chill.

2. Meanwhile, cook the potatoes in a large saucepan of salted, boiling water for 12–15 minutes until tender to the point of a knife, then drain well.

3. Drain the livers and pat dry. Season to taste. Heat the oil in a large frying pan set over a moderate heat.

4. Fry the garlic and livers for 2–3 minutes, tossing occasionally, until the livers are golden and firm.

5. Toss with the tomatoes, potatoes, salad, tarragon and seasoning; arrange on plates.

6. Whisk the yoghurt with the mustard and seasoning. Serve in pots on the side.

Crunchy Squid Salad

Serves: 4
Preparation time: 10–15 minutes
Cooking time: 10 minutes

Ingredients

2 tbsp coconut oil, melted

300 g / 10 ½ oz / 2 cups squid tubes,
  roughly chopped

225 g / 8 oz / 2 cups asparagus spears,
  woody ends removed

1 orange

1 tsp Dijon mustard

75 ml / 3 fl. oz / ⅓ cup olive oil

a small bunch of flat-leaf parsley,
  roughly chopped

100 g / 3 ½ oz / 2 cups beansprouts

75 g / 3 oz / 1 ½ cups baby spinach

1 pink grapefruit, peeled and segmented

salt and freshly ground black pepper

Method

1. Heat the oil in a large sauté pan set over
   a moderate heat until hot. Season the
   squid and add to the pan, sautéing for 3–4
   minutes until golden.

2. Drain on kitchen paper and set to one side.
   Meanwhile, cook the asparagus in a large
   saucepan of salted, boiling water for 2–3
   minutes until tender.

3. Drain and refresh in iced water. Juice and
   zest the orange into a small bowl before
   whisking in the mustard and then the olive
   oil until thickened.

4. Toss the squid and asparagus with
   the parsley, beansprouts, spinach and
   grapefruit.

5. Drizzle over the dressing before serving on
   plates with the rest of the dressing on
   the side.

Lamb Chop Salad

Serves: 4
Preparation time: 10 minutes
Cooking time: 15 minutes

Ingredients

4 x 150 g / 5 oz lamb chops on the bone, trimmed

2 tbsp coconut oil, melted

½ pomegranate

2 large clementines, peeled and segmented

1 large head radicchio, roughly chopped

55 g / 2 oz / 1 cup watercress, roughly torn

flaked sea salt and freshly ground black pepper

Method

1. Heat a griddle pan over a moderate heat until hot. Rub the lamb chops with coconut oil and season with salt and pepper.

2. Cook on the griddle pan for 8–10 minutes, turning occasionally, until charred and firm to the touch.

3. Hold the pomegranate half over a bowl and tap on its back with a wooden spoon to release the seeds.

4. Toss the seeds with the clementine segments, radicchio and watercress before arranging on plates.

5. Serve the lamb chops over the salad.

Tuna Tomato Salad

Serves: 4
Preparation time: 10 minutes
Cooking time: 10 minutes

Ingredients

400 g / 14 oz / 1 ¾ cups piece of tuna

2 tbsp olive oil

salt and freshly ground black pepper

225 g / 8 oz / 2 cups green (string) beans, trimmed

250 g / 9 oz / 1 ⅔ cups canned sardine fillets, drained

4 vine tomatoes, cored and sliced

1 large Romaine lettuce, chopped

1 red onion, thinly sliced

a small bunch of flat-leaf parsley, chopped

Method

1. Preheat the grill to a moderately hot temperature; drizzle the tuna with olive oil and season with salt and pepper.

2. Arrange on a tray and grill for 5–6 minutes, turning occasionally, until firm to the touch.

3. Remove from the grill and set to one side to cool. Cut into bite-size pieces.

4. Cook the beans in a large saucepan of salted, boiling water for 2–3 minutes until tender; drain and refresh in iced water.

5. Toss the cooked beans with the sardines, tomato, lettuce, onion and parsley and then arrange on serving plates.

6. Top with the grilled tuna, then serve.

Walnut Chicken Salad

Serves: 4
Preparation time: 10 minutes
Cooking time: 25–30 minutes

Ingredients

4 small skinless chicken breasts, sliced

2 tbsp olive oil

225 g / 8 oz / 2 cups walnuts, soaked in water for 20 minutes before draining

1 large onion, chopped

2 cloves of garlic, chopped

1 lemon, cut into wedges

a large bunch of flat-leaf parsley, roughly chopped

salt and freshly ground black pepper

Method

1. Preheat the oven to 190°C (170°C fan) / 375F / gas 5 and line a baking tray with greaseproof paper.

2. Toss the chicken slices with olive oil and seasoning. Spread out on the baking tray and roast for 18–22 minutes until cooked through.

3. Meanwhile, pulse together the walnuts, onion, and garlic with most of the parsley and some seasoning until pasty in texture.

4. Remove the chicken from the oven after 10 minutes and top with the walnut mixture.

5. Return to the oven for 8–12 minutes.

6. Remove from the oven and divide between plates before serving with lemon wedges and more parsley.

Pickled Herring Salad

Serves: 4
Preparation time:
20 minutes plus steeping
Cooking time: 20 minutes

Ingredients

500 ml / 18 fl. oz / 2 cups water

250 ml / 9 fl. oz / 1 cup distilled vinegar

6 herring fillets, pin-boned and descaled

150 g / 5 oz / 1 cup new potatoes, halved

75 g / 3 oz / ⅓ cup dairy-free coconut milk yoghurt

a small bunch of dill, roughly chopped

1 small red onion, sliced into rings

2 tbsp gherkin slices in vinegar, drained

1 large apple, cored and chopped

1 tsp red peppercorns, lightly crushed

Method

1. Bring the water and vinegar to a simmer in a large saucepan; add the herring and remove from the heat.

2. Cover and leave to steep for 1 hour. Meanwhile, cook the new potatoes in a large saucepan of salted, boiling water for 15–18 minutes, until tender.

3. Drain and leave to cool, then cut in half.

4. Drain the herring and pat dry then arrange on a serving plate.

5. Stir together the yoghurt, potatoes, most of the dill, red onion, gherkin and apple before spooning on top of the herring fillets.

6. Garnish with the remaining dill and peppercorns before serving.

Rabbit Leg Salad

Serves: 4
Preparation time: 10–15 minutes
Cooking time: 55–60 minutes

Ingredients

450 g / 1 lb / 3 cups baby turnips, halved

2 skinless rabbit legs, trimmed

2 tbsp coconut oil, melted

450 g / 1 lb / 3 cups cooked beetroot, quartered

150 g / 5 oz / 1 cup cooked golden beetroot, roughly chopped

salt and freshly ground black pepper

55 g / 2 oz / ½ cup pine nuts

2 tbsp pumpkin seeds

1 tbsp balsamic vinegar

200 g / 7 oz / 4 cups mixed leaf salad

Method

1. Preheat the oven to 180°C (160°C fan) / 350F / gas 4. Cook the turnip in a large saucepan of salted, boiling water for 8–10 minutes, then drain and leave to cool.

2. Rub the rabbit legs with the coconut oil and sit them in a roasting dish along with the beetroots and turnip; season generously.

3. Roast for 40–50 minutes until the rabbit is cooked through and registers at least 71°C / 160F on a thermometer.

4. Toast the pine nuts and pumpkin seeds in a dry frying pan over a moderate heat; add the vinegar and reduce until sticky.

5. Arrange the salad on a serving platter; serve the rabbit and vegetables over it with the pine nuts and pumpkin as well.

Tuna Tataki Salad

Serves: 4
Preparation time: 10-15 minutes
Cooking time: 15 minutes

Ingredients

110 ml / 4 fl. oz / ½ cup coconut oil, melted

a small bunch of coriander (cilantro), chopped

4 cloves of garlic, chopped

salt and freshly ground black pepper

500 g / 1 lb 2 oz of tuna

110 g / 4 oz / 1 cup asparagus spears, woody ends removed

1 Iceberg lettuce, roughly chopped

2 tbsp pine nuts

55 g / 2 oz / 1 cup salad cress, picked

150 g / 5 oz / 1 cup baby plum tomatoes, sliced

Method

1. Pulse together 75 ml / 3 fl. oz / ⅓ cup of the coconut oil with the coriander, garlic and seasoning; set to one side.

2. Preheat the grill to moderately hot. Brush the tuna fillet with the remaining oil, then season generously with salt and plenty of black pepper.

3. Grill for 6–8 minutes, turning once, until the tuna feels firm yet slightly springy; remove from the grill and cut into pieces.

4. Cook the asparagus in a saucepan of salted, boiling water for 2–3 minutes until tender before refreshing in iced water.

5. Drain and chop the asparagus before tossing with the lettuce, pine nuts, cress and tomatoes. Serve with slices of tuna and the dressing.

Chicken Walnut Salad

Serves: 4
Preparation time: 10 minutes
Cooking time: 10 minutes

Ingredients

2 tbsp coconut oil, melted

2 large skinless chicken breasts, diced

1 tsp paprika

salt and freshly ground black pepper

1 large carrot, peeled

1 round lettuce, chopped

200 g / 7 oz / 1 ⅓ cups green seedless
  grapes, halved

75 g / 3 oz / ¾ cup walnuts, roughly chopped

Method

1. Heat the coconut oil in a large frying pan
   set over a moderate heat until hot.

2. Season the chicken with paprika, salt
   and pepper before sautéing in the oil for
   7–8 minutes, tossing occasionally, until
   cooked through.

3. Pass the carrot over a mandolin with a
   julienne setting attached.

4. Arrange the chopped lettuce on plates and
   top with the carrot, grapes and walnuts.

5. Sit the chicken on top before serving.

Main Meals

Paleolithic foods offer you so much choice at dinner time – or at midday if that is when you eat your main meal. You can go for a simple grilled steak with steamed broccoli or try these more adventurous dishes which require minimal effort. Cooking the Paleolithic way is easy and tasty.

It helps to plan in advance so you know you are getting an interesting and varied mix of foods. As a rule of thumb, aim for one-third protein (meat, fish), just under two-thirds vegetables, and a good helping of fats (from nuts, avocado, eggs and olive oil). Cook using olive oil, coconut oil or animal fats.

Play around with menus and ideas. These delicious recipes show you how to experiment with different combinations. Don't stress if you also add in something that is not strictly Paleolithic. Remember the 80:20 balance, which allows you to go 'off menu' at times.

Roast Chicken Drumsticks

Serves: 4
Preparation time: 10–15 minutes
Cooking time: 45–50 minutes

Ingredients

4 onions, sliced

2 cloves of garlic, minced

2 spring onions (scallions), sliced

4 plum tomatoes, cored and diced

2 tbsp coconut oil, melted

2 tbsp balsamic vinegar

1 tbsp tomato purée

salt and freshly ground black pepper

8 small chicken drumsticks, trimmed

Method

1. Preheat the oven to 180°C (160°C fan) / 350F / gas 4.

2. Toss the onion, garlic, most of the spring onion and most of the tomato with the coconut oil, vinegar, tomato purée and seasoning.

3. Arrange in the base of a roasting dish and top with the chicken drumsticks.

4. Roast for 45–50 minutes until golden. Remove from the oven and leave to cool briefly before serving with the remaining spring onion and tomato as a garnish.

Osso Bucco

Serves: 4
Preparation time: 15 minutes
Cooking time:
2 hours 10–25 minutes

Ingredients

750 g / 1 lb 10 oz / 5 cups oxtail pieces

2 tbsp coconut oil, melted

salt and freshly ground black pepper

300 g / 10 ½ oz / 2 cups baby turnips, peeled and halved

300 g / 10 ½ oz / 2 cups baby carrots, peeled

125 g / 4 ½ oz / 1 cup mangetout

4 large spring onions (scallions), halved

250 ml / 9 fl. oz / 1 cup almond milk

a few sprigs of chervil, to garnish

Method

1. Preheat the oven to 180°C (160°C fan) / 350F / gas 4. Rub the oxtail pieces with the coconut oil before seasoning.

2. Sit the oxtail in a roasting dish and cover with aluminium foil; roast for 1 ¾–2 hours until the oxtail registers at least 66°C / 150F on a thermometer.

3. Remove and leave to rest, covered, for 15 minutes.

4. Cook the turnip and carrot in a saucepan of salted, boiling water for 8–10 minutes until tender; add the mangetout and spring onion 2 minutes before the root vegetables are cooked.

5. Drain and place in a saucepan with the almond milk. Bring to a simmer and season to taste before serving with the oxtail and chervil.

Roasted Pheasant Legs

Serves: 4
Preparation time: 15 minutes
Cooking time: 1 hour

Ingredients

3 tbsp olive oil

a small handful of flat-leaf parsley,
  finely chopped

6 cloves of garlic, minced

salt and freshly ground black pepper

2 large pheasant legs, trimmed

4 large carrots, peeled and sliced

4 Golden Delicious apples, cored and sliced

2 fennel bulbs, chopped

2 bay leaves

Method

1. Preheat the oven to 190°C (170°C fan) /
   375F / gas 5. Mash together the olive oil,
   parsley and garlic with salt and pepper.

2. Stuff the mixture under the skin of the
   pheasant legs. Arrange the carrots, apple,
   fennel and bay leaves in a roasting dish.

3. Sit the stuffed pheasant legs on top and
   cover with a sheet of kitchen foil. Roast for
   30 minutes before removing the foil.

4. Continue to roast for 25–30 minutes until
   the pheasant legs are cooked through.

5. Remove from the oven and leave to rest for
   5 minutes before serving.

Chicken Colombo

Serves: 4
Preparation time: 10 minutes
Cooking time: 30–35 minutes

Ingredients

2 tbsp coconut oil, melted

2 green chillies (chilies), sliced

4 small skinless chicken breasts, diced

salt and freshly ground black pepper

1 butternut squash, deseeded and diced

4 spring onions (scallions), sliced

a small bunch of thyme

500 ml / 18 fl. oz / 2 cups chicken stock

2 tsp wholegrain mustard

Method

1. Heat the oil in a casserole dish set over a moderate heat; add the chilli and sauté for 2 minutes, then add the chicken and some seasoning.

2. Cook for 4–5 minutes until browned all over.

3. Add the butternut squash, spring onions, thyme and stock. Bring to boiling point, then cook over a reduced heat for 20–25 minutes, until the squash is soft.

4. Stir through the mustard and season to taste before serving.

Warm Pigeon Salad

Serves: 4
Preparation time: 10–15 minutes
Cooking time: 15 minutes

Ingredients

4 large pigeon breasts, trimmed

2 tbsp olive oil

salt and freshly ground black pepper

2 large carrots, peeled and cut into batons

½ Savoy cabbage, shredded

375 ml / 13 fl. oz / 1 ½ cups chicken stock

225 g / 8 oz / 1 ½ cups prawns (shrimp), peeled

1 lime, cut into thin wedges

Method

1. Rub the pigeon breasts with olive oil, then season with salt and pepper and preheat a sauté pan over a moderate heat until hot.

2. Sear the breasts until golden all over, then remove from the pan and add the carrot, cabbage and seasoning.

3. Cook for 2 minutes, then cover with the stock.

4. Return the pigeon to the pan along with the prawns. Cover and cook for 4–5 minutes until the breasts are firm to the touch and the prawns are tender.

5. Add the lime wedges and season to taste. Slice the pigeon before serving over the cabbage and prawns.

Hazelnut-coated Chicken

Serves: 4
Preparation time: 15 minutes
Cooking time: 20 minutes

Ingredients

4 small skinless chicken breasts,
    cut into strips

2 tbsp hazelnut (cobnut) flour

salt and freshly ground black pepper

2 large eggs, beaten

100 g / 3 ½ oz / 1 cup hazelnuts (cobnuts),
    crushed

2 tbsp coconut oil, melted

150 g / 5 oz / 3 cups mixed leaf salad

75 g / 3 oz / ½ cup radishes, thinly sliced

Method

1. Preheat the oven to 200°C (180°C fan) /
   400F / gas 6. Dust the chicken strips with
   the flour and season generously.

2. Dip in the egg and let the excess drip off
   before coating in the crushed hazelnuts.
   Arrange on a baking tray.

3. Drizzle with coconut oil and bake for 15–18
   minutes until golden and cooked through.

4. Remove from the oven and leave to cool
   briefly. Arrange the mixed leaf salad and
   radish on plates and top with the chicken
   strips before serving.

Lamb Chops

Serves: 4
Preparation time: 10 minutes
Cooking time: 25 minutes

Ingredients

750 g / 10 ½ oz / 5 cups pumpkin,
  diced evenly

4 x 150 g / 5 oz lamb chops on the bone,
  cleaned and trimmed

2 tbsp almond butter

55 ml / 2 fl. oz / ¼ cup olive oil

salt and freshly ground black pepper

55 g / 2 oz / 1 cup baby spinach, washed

Method

1. Preheat the oven to 200°C (180°C fan) /
   400F / gas 6 and then line a baking tray
   with greaseproof paper.

2. Cook the pumpkin in a large saucepan of
   salted, boiling water for 18–22 minutes until
   tender. Brush the lamb chops with half of
   the olive oil before seasoning.

3. Arrange on the tray and roast for
   14–16 minutes until cooked, turning
   halfway through.

4. Drain the pumpkin and mash with the
   almond butter and seasoning until smooth.
   Remove the lamb and leave to rest,
   covered loosely, for 5 minutes.

5. Spoon the mash onto plates and serve with
   the lamb chops, spinach and remaining
   olive oil as a garnish.

Tuna Ratatouille

Serves: 4
Preparation time: 15 minutes
Cooking time: 30 minutes

Ingredients

3 tbsp olive oil

1 large onion, finely chopped

2 cloves of garlic, minced

2 large courgettes (zucchinis), diced

400 g / 14 oz / 2 cups canned chopped tomatoes

150 g / 5 oz / 1 ½ cups mangetout

salt and freshly ground black pepper

4 x 200 g / 7 oz tuna steaks

1 lemon, cut into wedges

a small bunch of basil leaves, picked

Method

1. Heat the oil in a large saucepan set over a medium heat until hot; add the onion, garlic and a little salt and sweat for 5–6 minutes.

2. Add the courgette and continue to cook for two minutes before covering with the chopped tomatoes.

3. Stir well and bring to a simmer, cooking steadily for 6 8 minutes until the courgette is tender; add the mangetout after 5 minutes.

4. Season to taste and set to one side. Preheat the grill to hot.

5. Season the tuna steaks and grill for 7–8 minutes, turning once halfway through.

6. Spoon the ratatouille into bowls and sit the tuna on top. Garnish with basil leaves and lemon wedges.

Chicken Casserole

Serves: 4
Preparation time: 10–15 minutes
Cooking time: 45–50 minutes

Ingredients

2 tbsp coconut oil, melted

2 onions, sliced

2 cloves of garlic, chopped

1 kg / 2 lb 4 oz chicken, trimmed and jointed

350 g / 12 oz / 2 ⅓ cups French breakfast radishes

750 ml / 1 pint 6 fl. oz / 3 cups chicken stock

salt and freshly ground black pepper

Method

1. Preheat the oven to 190°C (170°C fan) / 375F / gas 5.

2. Heat the oil in a casserole dish set over a moderate heat until hot. Add the onion, garlic and a little salt, sautéing for 4–5 minutes until lightly browned.

3. Add the chicken and continue to cook until browned all over; add the radish and stock and bring to a simmer.

4. Cover with a lid and transfer to the oven; cook for 35–40 minutes until the chicken pieces are cooked through.

5. Season to taste before serving.

Asian Veal Salad

Serves: 4
Preparation time: 10–15 minutes
Cooking time: 10 minutes

Ingredients

55 ml / 2 fl. oz / ¼ cup coconut oil, melted

salt and freshly ground black pepper

400 g / 14 oz piece of veal fillet, trimmed

2 pak choi, roughly chopped

1 large orange pepper, deseeded and sliced

1 courgette (zucchini), finely sliced

2 tbsp rice wine vinegar

1 tbsp black sesame seeds

a small bunch of coriander (cilantro), torn

Method

1. Heat half of the oil in a wok set over a high heat until hot. Season the veal, then seal for 1 minute on each side.

2. Remove from the pan and reduce the heat slightly before adding the rest of the oil.

3. Add the pak choi, pepper, courgette and seasoning; stir-fry for 3–4 minutes until softened.

4. Add the rice wine vinegar. Reduce by half, then season the stir-fry with salt and pepper.

5. Lift the stir-fry onto plates and slice the veal. Sit the veal on top and garnish with sesame seeds and coriander before serving.

Grilled Turkey Escalopes

Serves: 4
Preparation time: 10–15 minutes
Cooking time: 15 minutes

Ingredients

4 large turkey escalopes, trimmed

75 ml / 3 fl. oz / ⅓ cup olive oil

1 large courgette (zucchini),
   cut into long strips

2 red peppers, deseeded and sliced

225 g / 8 oz / 2 cups white asparagus spears,
   woody ends removed

salt and freshly ground black pepper

Method

1. Preheat a griddle pan over a moderate heat
   until hot. Drizzle the turkey with a little oil
   and season to taste.

2. Toss the vegetables with the remaining
   olive oil and season, then set to one side.

3. Cook the turkey for 5–6 minutes,
   turning occasionally, until cooked through.
   Remove from the pan and leave to rest in
   a warm place.

4. Add the vegetables to the pan and cook
   for 5–6 minutes, tossing occasionally, until
   lightly marked and tender.

5. Serve the vegetables with the cooked
   escalopes.

Tray Bake Chicken

Serves: 6
Preparation time: 10–15 minutes
Cooking time: 55–60 minutes

Ingredients

4 chicken legs, trimmed

2 heads of garlic, split in half

450 g / 1 lb / 3 cups carrots, peeled

350 g / 12 oz / 2 ⅓ cups parsnips, peeled and roughly sliced

600 g / 1 lb 5 oz / 4 cups turnips, peeled and chopped

55 ml / 2 fl. oz / ¼ cup olive oil

2 tbsp balsamic vinegar

salt and freshly ground black pepper

Method

1. Preheat the oven to 180°C (160°C fan) / 350F / gas 4.

2. Arrange the chicken legs, garlic, carrots, parsnips and turnips in a large roasting tray.

3. Add the olive oil and vinegar; toss well and season.

4. Cover the dish with kitchen foil. Roast for 30 minutes; discard the foil and continue to roast for a further 20–25 minutes until the legs are cooked through.

5. Remove from the oven and leave to rest briefly before serving.

Monkfish Rolls

Serves: 4
Preparation time: 10–15 minutes
Cooking time: 25 minutes

Ingredients

600 g / 1 lb 5 oz monkfish tail fillet

3 tbsp olive oil

a small bunch of thyme sprigs, roughly
  chopped

1 courgette (zucchini), finely sliced into strips

2 vine tomatoes, cored and sliced

1 lemon, finely sliced

salt and freshly ground black pepper

100 g / 3 ½ oz / ⅔ cup prosciutto slices

2 star anise

1 tsp fennel seeds

Method

1. Preheat the oven to 200°C (180°C fan) /
   400F / gas 6 and line a large baking tray
   with greaseproof paper.

2. Butterfly the monkfish tail and rub the
   inside with 1 tbsp of oil. Top with some
   thyme, courgette, tomato and lemon slices
   before seasoning generously.

3. Fold the monkfish around the filling and
   rub the outside with the remaining olive oil,
   then wrap with slices of prosciutto.

4. Sit on the baking tray and top with the star
   anise and fennel seeds. Roast for 18–20
   minutes until the fish is firm yet slightly
   springy to the touch.

5. Leave to rest briefly before serving with the
   remaining thyme as a garnish.

Wrapped Squash

Serves: 4
Preparation time: 10 minutes
Cooking time: 45–50 minutes

Ingredients

1 acorn or kabocha squash, cut into five wedges

55 ml / 2 fl. oz / ¼ cup olive oil

1 tsp dried thyme

½ tsp dried oregano

salt and freshly ground black pepper

10 rashers of streaky bacon

2 red onions, quartered

Method

1. Preheat the oven to 190°C (170°C fan) / 375F / gas 5.

2. Rub the wedges of squash with some olive oil, then season with the dried herbs, salt and pepper.

3. Wrap each wedge with a couple of rashers of bacon, then position in a roasting dish; tuck the red onion in and around the dish.

4. Drizzle with the remaining oil before seasoning. Roast for 40–45 minutes until the squash is tender.

5. Leave to cool slightly before serving.

Beef and Carrot Stew

Serves: 4
Preparation time: 15 minutes
Cooking time: 1 hour
30–35 minutes

Ingredients

3 tbsp coconut oil, melted

750 g / 1 lb 10 oz / 5 cups beef stewing
steak, cubed

salt and freshly ground black pepper

450 g / 1 lb / 3 cups carrots,
peeled and halved

350 g / 12 oz / 2 ⅓ cups parsnips,
peeled and halved

2 bay leaves

a small bunch of thyme

750 ml / 1 pint 6 fl. oz / 3 cups
light beef stock

Method

1. Preheat the oven to 180°C (160°C fan) /
350F / gas 4 and then heat 2 tbsp of the
coconut oil in a large casserole dish set
over a moderate heat.

2. Season the beef and seal in the oil until
golden all over. Remove from the dish and
add the remaining oil before reducing the
heat slightly.

3. Add the carrots, parsnips, bay leaves
and thyme; sauté for 4–5 minutes before
covering with the stock.

4. Bring to a simmer and cover with a lid.
Transfer to the oven for 1 hour 15–20
minutes until the beef is tender.

5. Season to taste before serving.

Stuffed Rolled Turkey

Serves: 4
Preparation time: 10 minutes
Cooking time: 55–60 minutes

Ingredients

110 g / 4 oz / 1 cup cashews, chopped

2 tbsp dried cranberries

2 small turkey breasts, trimmed and butterflied

a small handful of basil leaves

55 ml / 2 fl. oz / ¼ cup olive oil

salt and freshly ground black pepper

150 g / 5 oz / 1 ½ cups asparagus spears, woody ends removed

110 g / 4 oz / 1 cup green (string) beans, trimmed

350 g / 12 oz / 3 cups petit pois

2 Golden Delicious apples, halved

3 tbsp cranberry sauce

1 tbsp white sesame seeds

Method

1. Preheat the oven to 190°C (170°C fan) / 375F / gas 5.

2. Pulse together the cashews and cranberries. Layer the turkey breasts with basil leaves, then top with the nut and fruit mixture.

3. Roll up the breasts and secure with kitchen string. Arrange on a baking tray and drizzle with oil before seasoning. Roast for 40–45 minutes until the turkey is cooked through.

4. Cook the vegetables in a saucepan of salted, boiling water for 3 minutes. Drain and separate the petit pois before mashing with the rest of the oil and some seasoning.

5. Cut the rolled turkey and serve with the petit pois mash, asparagus, beans, apple and cranberry sauce; garnish with sesame seeds.

Summer Squid Salad

Serves: 4
Preparation time: 10 minutes
Cooking time: 10 minutes

Ingredients

400 g / 14 oz / 2 ⅔ cups baby squid, washed and dried

75 ml / 3 fl. oz / ⅓ cup olive oil

salt and freshly ground black pepper

2 courgettes (zucchinis)

100 g / 3 ½ oz / 1 ½ cups radishes

a small handful of tarragon, chopped

1 large orange, zested, peeled, segmented and chopped

2 tsp red peppercorns, lightly crushed

Method

1. Preheat the grill to hot. Drizzle the squid with half of the oil before seasoning.

2. Grill for 4–5 minutes, turning once, until tender.

3. Meanwhile, grate the courgette and radish on a mandolin with a julienne setting attached.

4. Pulse the remaining olive oil with the tarragon before tossing with the julienned vegetables.

5. Twirl the vegetables around a carving fork before sliding onto plates.

6. Top with the squid and serve with orange segments, orange zest and peppercorns to garnish.

Pumpkin and Cod Bake

Serves: 4
Preparation time: 10–15 minutes
Cooking time: 50–60 minutes

Ingredients

1.25 kg / 2 lb 12 oz / 8 cups culinary pumpkin, diced

55 g / 2 oz / ¼ cup dairy-free butter, cubed

salt and freshly ground black pepper

600 g / 1 lb 5 oz / 4 cups skinless cod fillet, pin-boned and diced

75 g / 3 oz / ¾ cup hazelnuts (cobnuts), chopped

a few sprigs of flat-leaf parsley, to garnish

Method

1. Cook the pumpkin in a large saucepan of salted, boiling water for 18–22 minutes until tender. Drain and leave to cool slightly, then mash with the butter and seasoning until smooth.

2. Preheat the oven to 190°C (170°C fan) / 375F / gas 5.

3. Arrange the cod in a round baking dish. Top with the pumpkin mash and smooth with the back of a tablespoon.

4. Sprinkle over the crushed hazelnuts and bake for 25–30 minutes until the nuts are toasted.

5. Remove from the oven and leave to cool before garnishing with parsley and serving.

Lamb Tagine

Serves: 4
Preparation time: 15 minutes
Cooking time: 1 ¾–2 hours

Ingredients

3 tbsp coconut oil, melted

salt and freshly ground black pepper

600 g / 1 lb 5 oz / 4 cups boneless lamb
  shoulder, diced

2 large onions, diced

4 cloves of garlic, chopped

2 tsp ras el hanout

100 g / 3 ½ oz / ⅔ cups pitted green olives

600 g / 1 lb 5 oz / 4 cups pumpkin, diced

500 ml / 18 fl. oz / 2 cups lamb stock

a large bunch of flat-leaf parsley, chopped

Method

1. Heat 2 tbsp of oil in a tagine or casserole
   dish set over a moderate heat.

2. Season the lamb before sealing in the hot
   oil until browned all over; remove from
   the tagine and reduce the heat a little
   underneath.

3. Add the remaining oil followed by the onion
   and garlic; sweat for 4–5 minutes until
   softened before adding the ras el hanout.

4. Cook for 1 minute, then add the olives,
   pumpkin and sealed lamb.

5. Pour over the stock and bring to a simmer;
   cover with a lid and cook over a low heat
   for 1 ½–1 ¾ hours until the lamb is tender.

6. Season to taste before serving with a
   garnish of parsley.

Stuffed Red Mullet

Serves: 4
Preparation time: 15 minutes
Cooking time: 20–25 minutes

Ingredients

3 lemons

4 whole red mullet, cleaned and gutted

a large bunch of tarragon

salt and freshly ground black pepper

55 ml / 2 fl. oz / ¼ cup extra-virgin olive oil

1 large cucumber, peeled, deseeded and sliced

150 g / 5 oz / 2 cups radishes, finely sliced

a small bunch of chives, finely chopped

Method

1. Preheat the oven to 190°C (170°C fan) / 375F / gas 5 and line a baking tray with greaseproof paper.

2. Slice 2 of the lemons and then stuff the mullet with the lemon slices and tarragon before seasoning.

3. Arrange on the lined tray and drizzle with half of the olive oil. Roast for 20–25 minutes until cooked through.

4. Zest and juice the remaining lemon into a mixing bowl; add the cucumber, radish and chives and remaining olive oil.

5. Toss well before seasoning to taste and then spoon into a serving bowl.

6. Serve the salad with the roasted mullet.

Snacks, Treats and Desserts

Even when it comes to snacks and tasty treats, it's easy to go Paleolithic. You will not be using cream and sugar but you will discover an array of alternatives.

Paleolithic desserts are quite delicious – think mousses, sorbets and luscious fruits. You'll undoubtedly want to make and sample some of these irresistible treats.

If you need a lift mid-afternoon, try healthy cookies or fruit crisps. Or reach for a banana, which is great for keeping energy levels balanced. For an anytime snack, grab a handful of nuts or seeds to munch – they're even tastier if you add some spice or toast them.

The occasional piece of good-quality dark chocolate will also do no harm – choose dark chocolate that has a 70 per cent or higher cocoa content.

Chocolate Mousse

Serves: 4
Preparation time: 10 minutes

Ingredients

400 g / 14 oz / 1 ¾ cups canned coconut
  milk, chilled overnight

3 tbsp cocoa powder

1 tbsp raw honey

½ tsp vanilla extract

Method

1. Open the can of coconut milk and scrape
   the hardened cream into a mixing bowl.

2. Beat with an electric mixer until smooth
   before adding the remaining ingredients.

3. Continue to beat until creamy and mousse-
   like in texture forms.

4. Divide between bowls and serve
   immediately.

Almond Butter Cookies

Makes: 16
Preparation time: 10 minutes
Cooking time: 25 minutes

Ingredients

225 g / 8 oz / 1 cup almond butter

2 tbsp raw honey

75 g / 3 oz / ½ cup coconut flour

1 large egg, beaten

½ tsp vanilla extract

a pinch of salt

2 tbsp flaked (slivered) almonds, to serve

250 ml / 9 fl. oz / 1 cup almond milk, to serve

Method

1. Preheat the oven to 180°C (160°C fan) / 350F / gas 4 and then line a baking tray with greaseproof paper.

2. Melt together the almond butter and honey in a saucepan. Leave to cool briefly, then fold through the coconut flour, beaten egg, vanilla extract and salt.

3. Take scoops of the dough and space apart on the tray; flatten slightly into rounds.

4. Bake for 15–18 minutes until golden and set, then remove to a wire rack to cool.

5. Garnish with flaked almonds and serve with almond milk.

Baked Apples and Pears

Serves: 4
Preparation time: 10 minutes
Cooking time: 40–50 minutes

Ingredients

150 ml / 5 fl. oz / ⅔ cup cold water

75 g / 3 oz / ⅓ cup raw honey

1 vanilla pod, split in half with seeds scraped out

2 Golden Delicious apples, split in half vertically

2 Conference pears, peeled and split in half vertically

Method

1. Preheat the oven to 180°C (160°C fan) / 350F / gas 4.

2. Combine the water, honey and vanilla seeds in a small saucepan; whisk briefly, then cook over a medium heat until dissolved and bubbling.

3. Continue to cook until the syrup has reduced by one-third for approximately 5 minutes.

4. Arrange the halved apples and pears in a small baking dish and pour over the syrup.

5. Roast the fruit for 30–40 minutes until tender. Remove from the oven and leave to cool slightly before serving.

Mixed Berry Sorbet

Serves: 4
Preparation time:
  10 minutes plus freezing
Cooking time: 5 minutes

Ingredients

250 ml / 9 fl. oz / 1 cup water
350 g / 12 oz / 2 ½ cups frozen mixed berries
2 tbsp raw honey

Method

1. Combine the water, berries and honey in a saucepan; cook over a medium heat until softened and thawed.
2. Pulse the mixture in a food processor until broken up, then allow it to cool.
3. Churn in an ice cream maker according to the manufacturer's instructions until frozen and set. Freeze for 2 hours.
4. Serve in tall glasses.

Chocolate Olive Mousses

Serves: 4

Preparation time:
  5–10 minutes plus freezing

Ingredients

400 g / 14 oz / 1 ¾ cups canned coconut
  milk, chilled overnight

55 ml / 2 fl. oz / ¼ cup extra-virgin olive oil

a pinch of salt

3 tbsp cocoa powder

1 ½ tbsp raw honey

1 orange

Method

1. Open the can of coconut milk and scrape
   the hardened cream into a mixing bowl.

2. Add most of the olive oil and beat with an
   electric mixer until thick and creamy; add
   the salt, cocoa powder and honey and
   continue to beat until mousse-like
   in texture.

3. Divide between pots, then cover and chill
   for 1 hour.

4. Before serving, pare the zest from the
   orange and finely slice. Toss with the
   remaining olive oil and serve over the
   mousses.

Nutty Baked Apples

Serves: 4
Preparation time: 10 minutes
Cooking time: 35–40 minutes

Ingredients

4 large Bramley apples

2 tbsp almonds, chopped

2 tbsp hazelnuts (cobnuts), chopped

1 tbsp pecans, chopped

1 tbsp walnuts, chopped

2 tbsp coconut oil, melted

1 tbsp mixed candied peel

2 tbsp raw honey

gluten-free gingerbread, to serve

Method

1. Preheat the oven to 180°C (160°C fan) / 350F / gas 4.

2. Remove the tops of the apples and scoop out a little of their cores; reserve the tops.

3. Mix together the nuts, coconut oil, candied peel and raw honey in a bowl, then spoon on top of the apples.

4. Sit the apples in a baking dish with their tops on the side.

5. Bake for 35–40 minutes until tender before removing and serving with gingerbread.

Figs and Sorbet

Serves: 4
Preparation time:
  5–10 minutes plus freezing

Ingredients

400 g / 14 oz / 2 cups canned peaches in
  juice, drained

400 ml / 14 fl. oz / 1 ¾ cups coconut water

450 g / 1 lb / 3 cups ripe figs, quartered

2 tbsp raw honey

Method

1. Purée the peaches in a food processor
   until smooth; add the coconut water and
   continue to process until smooth.

2. Pour into an ice cream maker and
   churn according to the manufacturer's
   instructions until frozen.

3. Freeze the sorbet for 2 hours.

4. Serve the sorbet over the figs with a drizzle
   of honey to garnish.

Pine Nut Cookies

Makes: 12
Preparation time: 15 minutes
Cooking time: 14–16 minutes

Ingredients

200 g / 7 oz / 1 ⅓ cups hazelnut
   (cobnut) flour
55 g / 2 oz / ½ cup pine nuts
55 g / 2 oz / ⅓ cup raisins
a pinch of salt
150 g / 5 oz / ⅔ cup coconut oil, melted
1 tbsp almond butter
1 tbsp raw honey
½ tsp vanilla extract

Method

1. Preheat the oven to 180°C (160°C fan) /
   350F / gas 4 and line a baking tray with a
   sheet of greaseproof paper.

2. Combine the flour, nuts, raisins and salt in a
   large mixing bowl then add the coconut oil,
   almond butter, honey and vanilla extract.

3. Mix well until you have a soft dough.

4. Take scoops of the dough and shape into
   fingers on the tray. Bake for 14–16 minutes
   until golden and set.

5. Remove to a wire rack to cool before
   serving.

Coconut Milk Panna Cottas

Makes: 4
Preparation time:
  5–10 minutes plus setting
Cooking time: 10 minutes

Ingredients

3 sheets of gelatine
500 ml / 18 fl. oz / 2 cups coconut milk
3 tbsp raw honey
1 lime, finely zested

Method

1. Soak the gelatine sheets in a small bowl of cold water and then combine the coconut milk and honey in a saucepan.

2. Cook over a medium heat until the honey has dissolved.

3. Remove the gelatine, squeezing out the excess water, then add to the hot coconut milk mixture.

4. Whisk briefly until the gelatine has dissolved, then set to one side to cool.

5. Divide between moulds then cover and chill for 3 hours, until set.

6. Before serving, warm the outsides of the moulds with a hot tea towel before turning onto plates and garnishing with lime zest.

Chestnut Pancakes

Serves: 4
Preparation time: 10 minutes
Cooking time: 20–25 minutes

Ingredients

125 g / 4 ½ oz / ¾ cup chestnut flour

a pinch of salt

2 medium eggs, beaten

250 ml / 9 fl. oz / 1 cup almond milk

1 tbsp raw honey

55 g / 2 oz / ¼ cup coconut oil, melted

150 g / 5 oz / 1 cup dairy-free coconut milk yoghurt, frozen

400 g / 14 oz / 2 cups canned cherries in juice, drained

Method

1. Combine the flour and salt in a mixing bowl. Whisk in the eggs, then add the milk gradually until smooth.

2. Whisk in the honey and 1 tbsp of oil; the rest of the oil will be used to grease the crepe pan between pancakes.

3. Heat a crêpe pan over a medium heat and grease; add a small ladle of batter and tilt the pan to let it spread out.

4. Cook for 1 minute until set, then flip and cook for a further 30 seconds before sliding onto a plate; repeat this method for the remaining pancakes, stacking once cooked.

5. Top the pancakes with cubes of frozen coconut yoghurt and cherries before serving.

Pumpkin Cake

Serves: 8
Preparation time: 15 minutes
Cooking time: 55–60 minutes

Ingredients

2 tbsp coconut oil, melted

250 g / 9 oz / 1 cup almond butter

3 tbsp raw honey

½ tsp ground cinnamon

½ tsp ground allspice

a pinch of salt

2 small pumpkins, peeled and cut into thin slices

a few sprigs of sage, to garnish

Method

1. Preheat the oven to 180°C (160°C fan) / 350F / gas 4. Grease and line an 18 cm (7 in) square cake tin with coconut oil and greaseproof paper.

2. Warm together the almond butter, honey, ground spices and salt in a small saucepan.

3. Layer slices of the pumpkin in the cake tin, pouring a little of the almond butter mixture between each layer.

4. Cover with foil and bake for 35–40 minutes until the pumpkin is tender.

5. Remove the foil and bake uncovered for a further 10 minutes until browned on top.

6. Remove to a wire rack to cool before turning out, slicing, and garnishing with sage.

Hazelnut Financiers

Makes: 18
Preparation time: 10 minutes
Cooking time: 15–18 minutes

Ingredients

200 g / 7 oz / 1 ⅓ cups hazelnut (cobnut) flour
a pinch of salt
110 g / 4 oz / ½ cup raw honey
5 medium egg whites
150 g / 5 oz / ⅔ cup coconut oil, melted
75 g / 3 oz / ¾ cup hazelnuts (cobnuts),
   chopped

Method

1. Preheat the oven to 200°C (180°C fan) /
   400F / gas 6.

2. Combine the hazelnut flour and salt in a
   large mixing bowl; add the honey and egg
   whites and mix well until combined.

3. Add the coconut oil and fold until
   incorporated. Spoon into a 24-hole
   financier mould and top with chopped
   hazelnuts.

4. Bake for 15–18 minutes until golden and
   risen, then remove to a wire rack to cool
   before turning out and serving.

Poached Spiced Pears

Serves: 4
Preparation time: 10 minutes
Cooking time: 30–35 minutes

Ingredients

2 large oranges

4 large pears, peeled, cored and quartered

1 cinnamon stick

1 tsp cloves

750 ml / 1 pint 6 fl. oz / 3 cups cold water

Method

1. Pare the zest from the oranges and julienne. Juice the oranges into a saucepan and add the zest.

2. Add the remaining ingredients and bring to a simmer. Cover with a lid and cook over a low heat for 25–30 minutes until the pears are tender to the tip of a knife.

3. Serve warm or cold.

Apple Crisps

Serves: 4
Preparation time: 10 minutes
Cooking time: 50–55 minutes

Ingredients

4 Golden Delicious apples
½ tsp salt

Method

1. Preheat the oven to 110°C (90°C fan) / 225F / gas ¼.

2. Thinly slice the apples on a mandolin into 5 mm (¼ in) slices; pat dry and arrange on large baking trays, spaced apart.

3. Sprinkle with a little salt then bake for 50–55 minutes until dried out.

4. Remove to a wire rack to cool before serving.

Rosemary Apricots

Serves: 4
Preparation time: 5–10 minutes
Cooking time: 30–40 minutes

Ingredients

800 g / 1 lb 12 oz / 4 cups canned apricot
halves in juice

55 ml / 2 fl. oz / ¼ cup lemon juice

½ tsp dried rosemary

4 sprigs of rosemary

Method

1. Preheat the oven to 180°C (160°C fan) /
350F / gas 4.

2. Neatly arrange the apricot halves and juice
in a roasting tin; stir in the lemon juice and
dried rosemary.

3. Tuck the rosemary sprigs in and around the
apricots.

4. Roast for 30–40 minutes until the apricots
are lightly browned on top.

5. Remove from the oven and leave the
apricots to cool a little before serving
in bowls.

Chocolate Loaves

Makes: 8
Preparation time: 10 minutes
Cooking time: 25–30 minutes

Ingredients

100 g / 3 ½ oz / ⅔ cup cocoa powder
100 g / 3 ½ oz / ⅔ cup coconut flour
55 g / 2 oz / ⅓ cup arrowroot
½ tsp baking powder
½ tsp bicarbonate of (baking) soda
5 large eggs
55 g / 2 oz / ¼ cup coconut oil, melted
150 g / 5 oz / ⅔ cup raw honey
1 tsp vanilla extract

Method

1. Preheat the oven to 160°C (140°C fan) / 325F / gas 3 and grease 8 individual loaf tins.

2. Sift together the cocoa powder, coconut flour, arrowroot, baking powder and bicarbonate of soda.

3. Beat together the eggs, coconut oil, honey and vanilla extract in a measuring jug, then add to the dry ingredients and fold through until incorporated.

4. Distribute the batter between the tins and arrange on a baking tray. Bake for 25–30 minutes until a cake tester comes out clean from their centres.

5. Remove to a wire rack to cool before serving.

Food Plan and Diary

Any new eating programme needs planning – otherwise you are likely to stop before you have really got started. Planning helps you stick to the diet, especially in the early days when you are adjusting to the 'can' and 'can't' foods.

Be realistic

The Paleolithic diet can take a little while to get used to – avoiding dairy, grains and processed foods may be especially difficult. Accept that sometimes you may eat something 'off menu'. The suggested 80:20 ratio gives you a little leeway. This new way of eating can be a long-term lifestyle choice, so it's OK to go non-Paleolithic from time to time.

In this section, you can plan your meals to make it easier to stick to the Paleolithic diet, especially when you first start. Think about your work, family or social commitments for each week and make the Paleolithic diet work for you. You can add in your exercise programme too, so you know what you are aiming to do.

Check it out

Take your time looking at the recipes in this book. Check out the Internet as well, as there is a vibrant, online Paleolithic community sharing tips and tasty meal ideas. Make a list and enjoy buying fresh from your local markets and farm shops, as well as supermarkets. Shopping around will keep the budget down too.

Week 1

	Breakfast	Lunch	Snack	Dinner
Monday				
Tuesday				
Wednesday				
Thursday				
Friday				
Saturday				
Sunday				

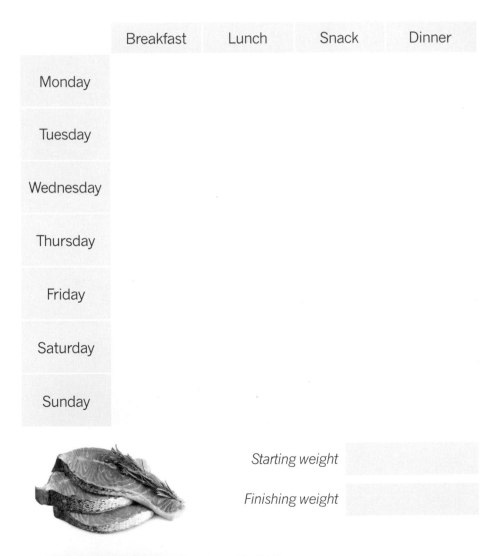

Starting weight

Finishing weight

Exercise log

How I feel

Week 2

	Breakfast	Lunch	Snack	Dinner
Monday				
Tuesday				
Wednesday				
Thursday				
Friday				
Saturday				
Sunday				

Starting weight

Finishing weight

Exercise log

How I feel

Week 3

	Breakfast	Lunch	Snack	Dinner
Monday				
Tuesday				
Wednesday				
Thursday				
Friday				
Saturday				
Sunday				

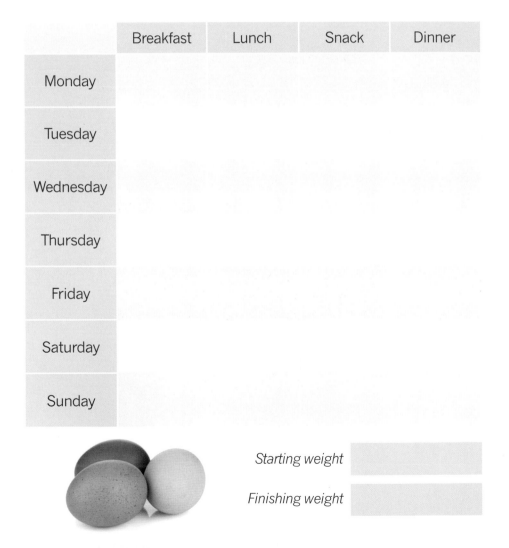

Starting weight

Finishing weight

Exercise log

How I feel

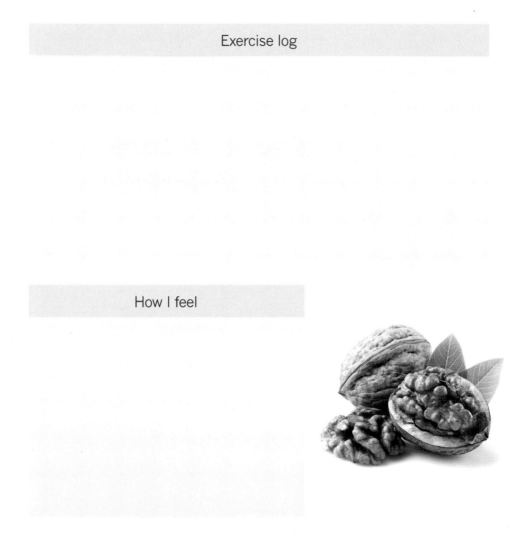

Week 4

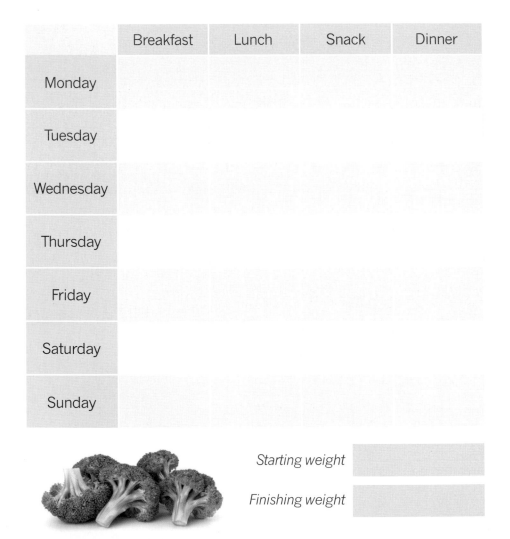

	Breakfast	Lunch	Snack	Dinner
Monday				
Tuesday				
Wednesday				
Thursday				
Friday				
Saturday				
Sunday				

Starting weight

Finishing weight

Exercise log

How I feel

A Paleolithic Kitchen

First of all you will need to sort out your kitchen. It's an opportunity to get rid of out-of-date bottles of sugary sauces or old bags of crumbly flour. You don't have to throw out all non-Paleolithic foods, but do put them at the back of a cupboard so you're not tempted to use them, particularly when you start out. Re-stock gradually with the foods listed opposite. Top tip to help you stay on track – don't food shop when you are hungry!

Equipment

You don't need special equipment but, if you don't have one already, invest in a small food processor or mixer so you can whizz up delicious dips.

Buy sticky labels so you can date and label food that you prepare and freeze.

It's also useful to have freezable containers of different sizes so you can easily freeze portions for one or two people, or more, depending on requirements. Handy containers are a must for taking lunch to work too.

Shopping list

Olive oil (extra virgin, if possible)

Coconut oil

Ghee (ghee is clarified butter, prepared by boiling butter and removing the milk solids. Buy it from supermarkets, or make your own)

Garlic

Fresh ginger

Raw local honey

Sea salt

Herbs and spices

Eggs

Lean meat – organic if possible – beef chicken, duck, pork

Fish – salmon, mackerel, haddock, sardines

Seafood – shrimps, prawns, squid, lobster, crab

Nuts – (except peanuts)

Seeds, such as sunflower, pumpkin and flaxseeds

Selection of Vegetables – organic if possible

Onions

Mushrooms

Leafy green vegetables

Carrots

Courgettes (zucchini)

Parsnips

Squashes – including pumpkin, butternut squash

Peppers

Tomatoes

Avocados

Fruit

Berries of many different varieties – blueberries, raspberries, strawberries, blackcurrants

Apples

Oranges

Lemons and limes (great for adding zest)

Melon

Apricots

Figs

Pineapple

Bananas

Grapefruit

Mango

At Work and Play

A healthy eating plan or diet is only going to work if it makes you feel good. Feeling good is about being fit and healthy, and also about having fun with friends and family. It's about general well-being – knowing that different parts of your life slot together easily. It's important to ensure that your new diet fits into your working and social life so you can enjoy both to the full.

Here's how to eat the Paleolithic way – sticking to all its general principles wherever you are and whatever you're doing – without becoming a diet bore.

Work

Take a packed lunch and snacks. If you and colleagues go out to eat, check out in advance what's on offer so you can make quick and easy choices. If there is a canteen, choose grilled meat or fish, and plain vegetables. If you find everything covered in processed sauces, have a word with the catering manager and suggest a few practical alternatives – your work colleagues will benefit too!

Family time

If you are the main cook at home, either introduce some Paleolithic meals to the weekly menu or make sure that you prepare a Paleolithic part to each meal so you don't have to make two separate meals.

Party time

No one wants to be a diet bore at a party or social gathering. If you know you are going out, plan ahead. Have a Paleolithic snack or light meal before you leave home, so you can then eat only the Paleolithic foods on offer while you are out. Alternatively, plan your social occasions as part of your permitted 20 per cent allowance. An occasional glass of red wine will do you or your diet no harm.

Staying Paleolithic

You've done the hard bit! You've planned, bought foods and started the diet. You are looking good and feeling good. So you probably won't want to change your eating patterns now. However, it takes a little effort to keep up the good work.

The following top tips will help you to stay on course, so that Paleolithic eating and all its benefits become a part of your life.

- Ask a partner or close friend to try out Paleolithic foods with you – they will most likely love them and become converts.

- Keep looking back at your aims and goals. Adapt them if they feel too unrealistic for the moment, then amend them later. If they feel too easy, then challenge yourself.

- Keep experimenting with new recipes and ingredients.

- Try out one new recipe or new food a week.

- Entertain in style. Surprise your friends with an amazingly tasty meal, Paleolithic style.

- Vary your exercise routine.

- On holiday, you may need to be flexible. Don't worry about it – just enjoy the time away and plan a routine for your return to ensure you stay motivated.

- Check out the Internet for new ideas and top tips.

- Make this diet your own. Adapt it to suit your lifestyle and body.

- Treat yourself in some way, such as having a luxurious massage. You deserve it.

Be kind to yourself

The most important thing to do is look after yourself. Now you've started the Paleolithic diet, enjoy its benefits and make it part of a happy, relaxed life.

Diet consultant: Jo Stimpson.

Written by: Ella Newell.

Main food photography and recipe development: PhotoCuisine UK.

Picture Credits

Dreamstime: 4 Mimagephotography, 6, 22 Monkey Business Images, 8 Ariwasabi, 9 Edyta Pawlowska, 11 Epicstock, 14t Eyewave, 14m Robyn Mackenzie, 14b Lockstockbob, 16 Evgeny Karandaev, 17 Viktorfischer, 19 Nyul, 21 Bevan Goldswain, 23 Prapass Wannapinij, 25 Pawel Papis, 27 Monkey Business Images Ltd, 29 Candybox Images, 30 Cenorman, 33 Hongqi Zhang (aka Michael Zhang), 36b Serhiy Shullye, 37b Cameramannz, 38b, 39b, 91b Olga Lupol, 40b Alexey Buhantsoff, 41b Valentyn75, 42b Lindavostrovska, 43b Ppy2010ha, 44b Skolton, 45b Joruba, 46b Dan82, 47b Rozum, 48b Yurakp, 49b Anna Sedneva, 50b Cristian Dina, 51b Yvdavyd, 54b Christian Draghici, 55b Artman, 56b Sergii Kolesnyk, 57b Nataliya Hora, 58b Angel Luis Simon Martin, 59b Anthony Baggett, 60b Stefanocar75, 61b Alexander Raths, 62b Levente Gyori, 79b Margo555, 80b Norman Chan, 81b Robyn Mackenzie, 89b Thodonal, 92b Ovydyborets, 96b Duskbabe, 97b Sommai Sommai, 98b Ekaterina Fribus, 99b Patricia Hofmeester, 100b Sak111, 101b Olga Vasileva, 102b Tadeusz Wejkszo, 103b Margouillat, 104b Vivilweb, 105b Kenzenbrv, 106b Evgeny Karandaev, 107b Artem Samokhvalov, 108b Svetlana Kuznetsova, 109b Peter Zijlstra, 110b Anna Kucherova, 111b HandmadePictures; Shutterstock: 13 Richard Griffin, 15 Kzenon, 31 Seregam, 64b Amero, 65b Valentyn Volkov, 66b Tim UR, 67b spline_x, 68b Volosina, 69b Anna Kucherova, 70b abc7, 71b Evgeny Karandaev, 74b studioVin, 75b Gyorgy Barna, 76b Hayati Kayhan, 77b zcw, 78b marilyn barbone, 82b andersphoto, 83b SOMMAI, 84b, 120 Nattika, 85b mario95, 86b Andrii Gorulko, 87b supakit hongsakul, 88b photogal, 90b Maks Narodenko, 93b Andris Tkacenko, 112b wavebreakmedia, 113 Boris Ryaposov, 114 geniuscook_com, 115, 119 Dionisvera, 116 Abel Tumik, 117 Volosina, 118 Evgeny Karandaev, 121 Africa Studio, 122 Andresr, 125 Matthew Ennis, 126 bikeriderlondon, 127 Mila Supinskaya, 128 Piotr Marcinski; Thinkstock: 14 bergamont.